ABC...123...Jesus Created Fruits & Vegetables & People like you and me.

English & Spanish

OCTOBER 4, 2023

ARTWORKS BY DONNA BURCH

About the Author

Donna J Burch is a published author of 22 books, including this one. She is an acrylic artist, teacher, gardener, community volunteer and retired bank officer.

She has also created a positive life group on Facebook (META) for women called **"BUCKET LIST OR NOT,"** that posts all positive sayings, photos, recipes, goals, events, get togethers, coffee groups, playing cards, dinners, games, luncheons, exercises and just plain having fun with new and old friends. This is a safe place for women to meet and go to feel awesome and get support from each other.

The group was created after she met her bucket list goal of writing and publishing her first book of "Come and Travel Cross Country with Donna and Russell!" It is all about planning and travelling to all of the states!

She recently published the 4th book in the Spy World Series. The first book is called "Once in a Lifetime Spies." You can check out her Facebook page called "SPY WORLD BY DONNA BURCH".
17 of her published books are written for children, teens and adults, 1 is the travel book and 4 are the Spy World Series.

All of the books can be purchased at www.amazon.com and www.barnesandnoble.com under the name of Donna Burch and are sold as hardcover, paperback and kindle. You may also have your local bookstore order them for you.

You can check out the author page at:
www.amazon.com/author/donnaburch.

ABC...123...Jesus Created Fruits & Vegetables & People like you and me.

Read and Count with me in English & Spanish

By Donna J Burch

Joel 1:3

Tell ye your children of it, and let your children tell their children, and their children another generation.

Learn how to say and count numbers,
colors, fruits & vegetables in English & Spanish

and

Meet people and learn verses in the Bible.

Each page will have a letter of the alphabet in order and there will be item(s) that begin with that letter. Colors will be listed in both English and Spanish. There will also be a person from the Bible that begins with that letter and verses in the Bible that have fruit in them.

This book is dedicated to my husband,
Russell Burch, who is always there for me.
He puts up with my craziness and my many
ideas and crafts. Thank you for loving me.
I love you to the moon and back. I also must thank
the Lord Jesus Christ for my life.

The book is for families to enjoy reading together.

A is for Apple

1 Apple

One Apple

Una manzana (Spanish)

Red (English)

Roja (Spanish)

Adam is the first man in the Bible in the Book of Genesis.

Song of Solomon 2:3c

As the apple tree among the trees of the wood, so is my beloved among the sons. I sat down under his shadow with great delight, and his fruit was sweet to my taste.

B is for Bananas

Two Bananas

2 Bananas

Dos Bananas (Spanish)

Yellow (English)

Amarilla (Spanish)

Barabbas was a prisoner in the New Testament.

Genesis 3:2

And the woman said unto the serpent, We may eat of the fruit of the trees of the garden:

C is for Cherries

Three Cherries

3 Cherries

Tres cerezas (Spanish)
Red (English)
Roja (Spanish)

Cain was a son of Adam and Eve

Leviticus 26:4C

<mark>Then I will give you rain in due season, and the land shall yield her increase, and the trees of the field shall yield their fruit.</mark>

D is for Dates

Four Dates

4 Dates

Cuatro fechas (Spanish)
Brown (English)
Marron (Spanish)

Daniel was a fallen angel in the Book of Enoch

Galatians 5:22

But the fruit of the Spirit is love, joy, peace, longsuffering, gentleness, goodness, faith,

E is for Eggplant

5 Eggplants

Five Eggplants

Cinco Berenjena (Spanish)

Purple (English)

Purpura (Spanish)

Eve was the first woman created in the Book of Genesis and Adam's wife

Mark 4:29c

But when the fruit is brought forth, immediately he putteth in the sickle, because the harvest is come.

F is for figs

6 figs

Six Figs

Seis Higos (Spanish)

Purple/green & pink (English)

Purpura/Verde/Rosado (Spanish)

Four Horsemen in the Book of Revelation

Judges 9:11

But the fig tree said unto them, Should I forsake my sweetness, and my good fruit, and go to be promoted over the trees?

G is for Grapefruit

Seven Grapefruit

7 Grapefruit

Siete toronjas (Spanish)

Yellow/Pink (English)

Amarillo/Rosado (Spanish)

Gabriel was an Angel

Matthew 13:8

But other fell into good ground, and brought forth fruit, some an hundredfold, some sixtyfold, some thirtyfold.

H is for Honeydew Melon

8 Honeydew Melons

Eight Honeydew Melons

Ocho Melones honeydew(Spanish)
Beige/Yellow (English)
Beige/Amarillo (Spanish)

Hadad is the son of Ishmael

Genesis :3

And in process of time it came to pass, that Cain brought of the fruit of the ground an offering unto the LORD.

I is for Ice Cubes

9 Ice Cubes

Nine Ice Cubes

Nueve Cubos de hielo (Spanish)

Clear (English)

Clara (Spanish)

Isaiah is a Hebrew Prophet

Proverbs 25:20c

As he that taketh away a garment in cold weather, and as vinegar upon nitre, so is he that singeth songs to an heavy heart.

J is for Java-Plum

10 Java-Plums

Ten Java-Plums

Diez Ciruelas java (Spanish)

Blue/purple (English)

Azul/Purpura (Spanish)

Jesus is the Son of God

Matthew 7:20

Wherefore by their fruits ye shall know them.

K is for Kiwifruit

11 Kiwifruit

Eleven Kiwifruit

Once Kiwis (Spanish)

Brown/Green (English)

Marron/Verde (Spanish)

Kokabiel is a fallen Angel

Matthew 7:16

Ye shall know them by their fruits. Do men gather grapes of thorns, or figs of thistles?

L is for Lemons

12 Lemons

Twelve Lemons

Doce Limones (Spanish)

Yellow (English)

Amarilla (Spanish)

Lamech is the father of Noah

Luke 12:17

And he thought within himself, saying, What shall I do, because I have no room where to bestow my fruits?

M is for Mangos

13 Mangos

Thirteen Mangos

Trece Mango (Spanish)

Red/Green (English)

Roja/Verde (Spanish)

Mary is the mother of Jesus

2 Timothy 2:6

The husbandman that laboureth must be first partaker of the fruits.

N is for Nectarines

14 Nectarines

Fourteen Nectarines

Catorce nectarinas (Spanish)

Red/Yellow (English)

Roja/Amarilla (Spanish)

Noah built the ark for the great flood

Ecclesiastes 2:5

I made me gardens and orchards, and I planted trees in them of all kind of fruits:

O is for Oranges

15 is for Oranges

Fifteen is for Oranges

Quince Naranjas (Spanish)

Orange (English)

Naranja (Spanish)

Obadiah was a Prophet

Ecclesiastes 2:5

I made me gardens and orchards, and I planted trees in them of all kind of fruits:

P is for Peaches

16 Peaches

Sixteen Peaches

Dieciseis Duraznos (Spanish)

Orange, red, peach (English)

Naranja/Roja/Melocoton (Spanish)

Peter was an Apostle and first Pope

Psalms 107:37

And sow the fields, and plant vineyards, which may yield fruits of increase.

Q is for Quince

17 Quince

Seventeen Quince

Diecisiete Membrillo (Spanish)

Yellow (English)

Amarillo (Spanish)

Queen of Sheba who tested Solomon's wisdom

Ecclesiastes 2:5

I made me gardens and orchards, and I planted trees in them of all kind of fruits:

R is for Raspberries

18 Raspberries

Eighteen Raspberries

Dieciocho frambuesas (Spanish)

Red (English)

Roja (Spanish)

Rachel is the wife of Jacob

Psalms 107:37

And sow the fields, and plant vineyards, which may yield fruits of increase.

S is for Strawberries

19 Strawberries

Nineteen Strawberries

Diecinueve Fresas (Spanish)

Red (English)

Roja (Spanish)

Samson had supernatural strength

Philippians 1:11

Being filled with the fruits of righteousness, which are by Jesus Christ, unto the glory and praise of God.

T is for Tangerine

20 Tangerines

Twenty Tangerines

Veinte Mandarinas (Spanish)

Orange (English)

Naranja (Spanish)

Tema is son of Ishmael

Exodus 23:10

And six years thou shalt sow thy land, and shalt gather in the fruits thereof:

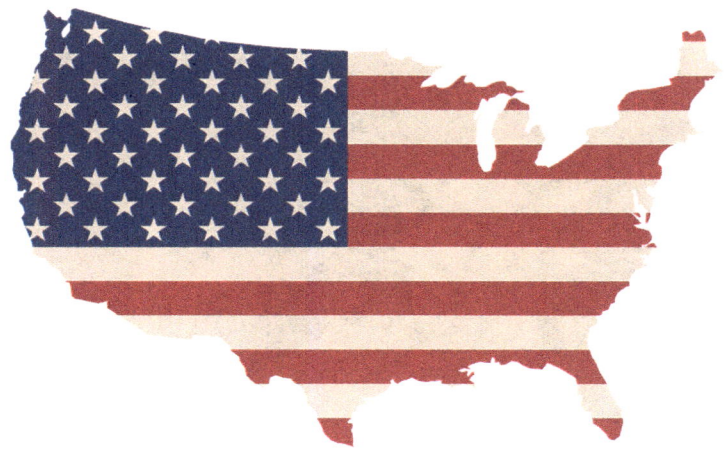

U is for United States

21 Stars

Twenty-one Stars

Veintiuno Estrellas (Spanish)
White (English)
Blanca (Spanish)

Uzziah was the King of Judah

Matthew 21:34

And when the time of the fruit drew near, he sent his servants to the husbandmen, that they might receive the fruits of it.

V is for Vegetables

22 Vegetables

Twenty-Two Vegetables

Veintidos Vegetales (Spanish)

Green/Yellow/Red/Orange (English)

Verde/Amarilla/Roja/Naranje (Spanish)

Vashti was the Queen of Persia

Matthew 21:43

Therefore say I unto you, The kingdom of God shall be taken from you, and given to a nation bringing forth the fruits thereof.

W is for Watermelon

23 Watermelon

Twenty-Three Watermelon

Veintitres Sandia (Spanish)

Green/Yellow (English)

Verde/Amarilla (Spanish)

Watcher was a fallen Angel

Job 31:39

If I have eaten the fruits thereof without money, or have caused the owners thereof to lose their life:

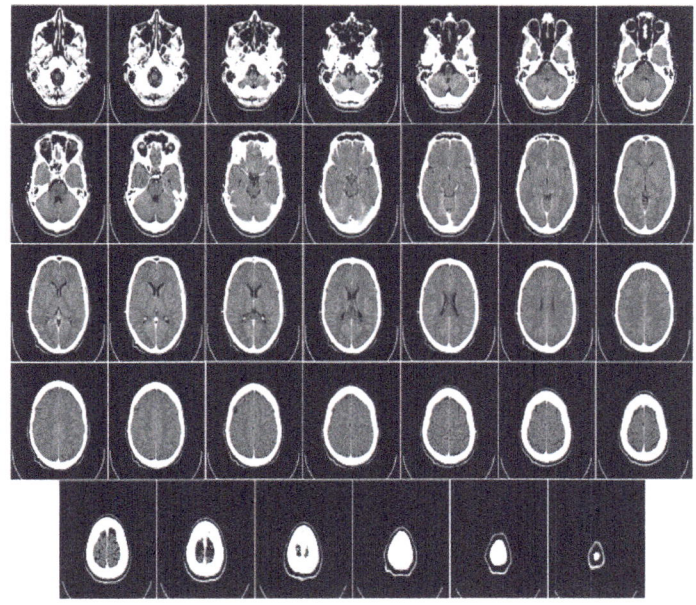

X is for Xrays

24 Xrays

Twenty-Four Xrays

Veinticuatro Rayos X

Black/White

Negra/Blanca

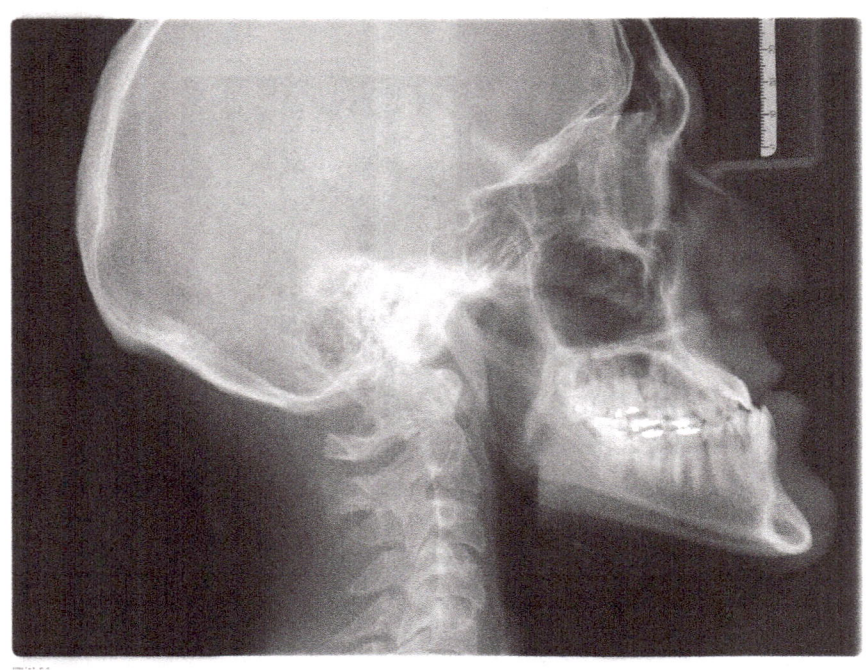

James 3:17

But the wisdom that is from above is first pure, then peaceable, gentle, and easy to be intreated, full of mercy and good fruits, without partiality, and without hypocrisy.

Y is for Yams

25 Yams

Twenty-Five Yams

Veinticinco Batatas (Spanish)
Red/Orange (English)
Roja/Naranje (Spanish)

Yomiel was a fallen Angel

Luke 12:18

And he said, This will I do: I will pull down my barns, and build greater; and there will I bestow all my fruits and my goods.

Z is for Zucchini

26 Zucchini

Twenty-Six Zucchini

Veintiseis Calabacin (Spanish)
Green (English)
Verde (Spanish)

Zechariah was a priest and husband of Elisabeth

Song of Solomon 6:11

I went down into the garden of nuts to see the fruits of the valley, and to see whether the vine flourished, and the pomegranates budded.

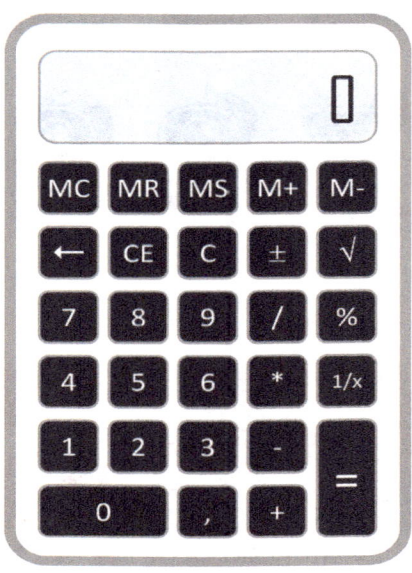

Verses are from the KJV Bible

B

_____

_____

_____

D

E

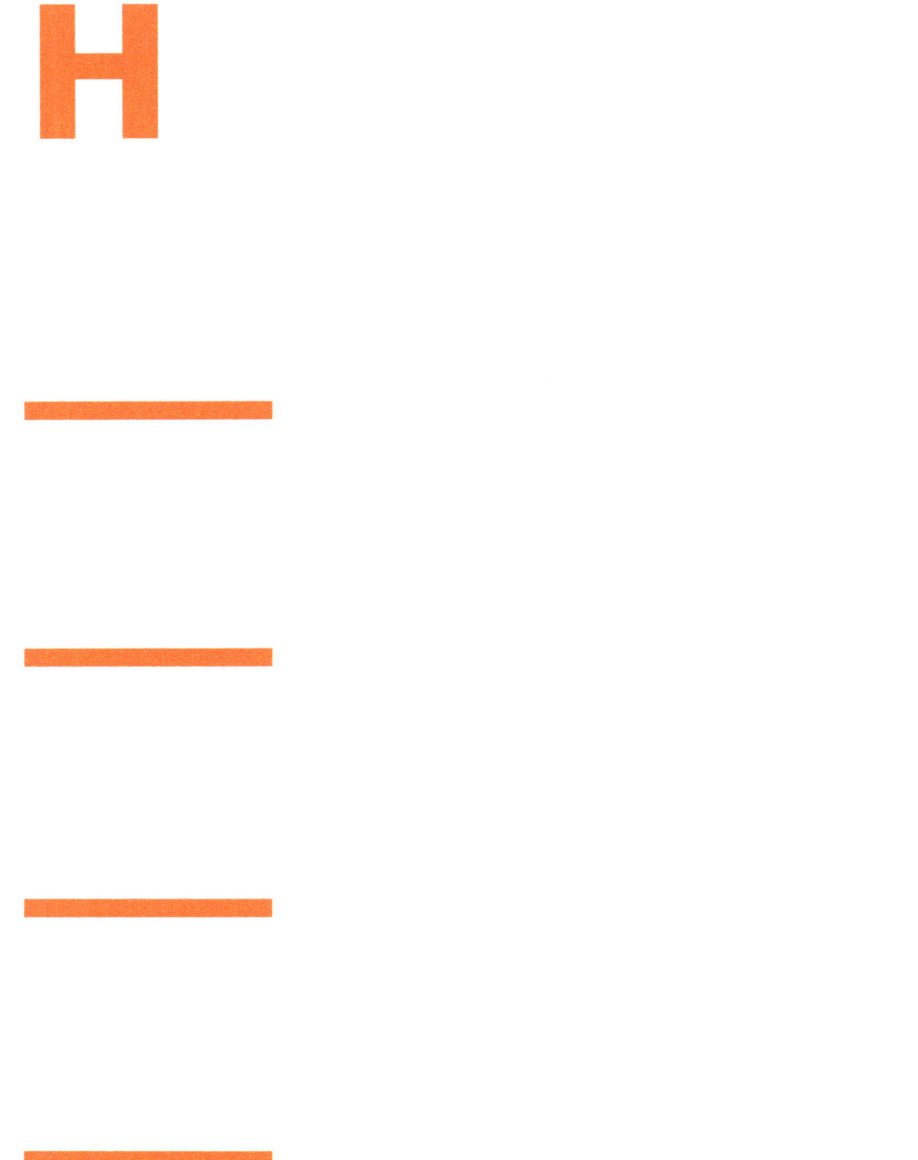

N

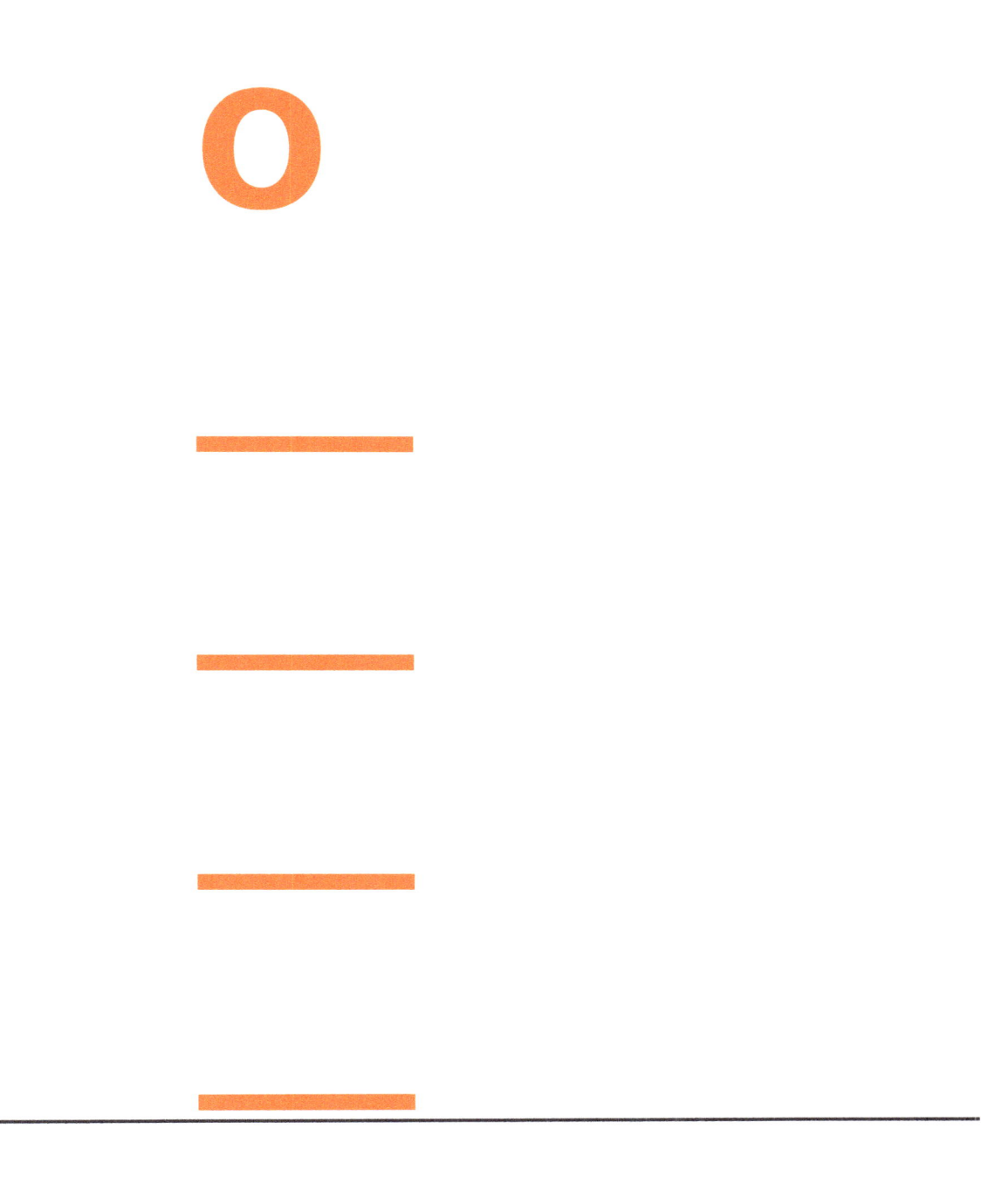

Q

_____

_____

_____

_____

S

Made in the USA
Monee, IL
24 October 2023

45041520R00050